Ancient
Egyptian Art

Susie Hodge

Heinemann Interactive Library

Des Plaines, Illinois

Published by Heinemann Interactive Library,
an imprint of Reed Educational & Professional Publishing,
1350 East Touhy Avenue, Suite 240 West,
Des Plaines, IL 60018

Designed by Plum Creative
Illustrations by Oxford Illustrators

Printed in Hong Kong / China

02 01 00 99 98
10 9 8 7 6 5 4 3 2

Library of Congress Cataloging-in-Publication Data
Hodge, Susie, 1960–
    Ancient Egyptian art / Susie Hodge.
      p. cm. -- (Art in history)
    Includes bibliographical references and index.
    Summary: Examines the art of ancient Egypt, including wall painting, reliefs, buildings, and sculpture.
    ISBN 1-57572-550-9 (lib. bdg.)
    1. Art. Egyptian--Juvenile literature.   2. Art, Ancient--Egypt-
-Juvenile literature. [1. Art, Egyptian. 2. Art, Ancient.]
I. Title. II. Series: Hodge, Susie, 1960– Art in history.
N5350.H63   1997
709'.32--dc21   97–20676
                              CIP
                              AC

Acknowledgments
The author and publisher are grateful to the following for permission to reproduce copyright photographs:
Ancient Art & Architecture Collection pp4, 6, 19; Bridgeman Art Library / Giraudon p13; British Museum pp5, 7, 9, 14–15, 17, 21, 24, 28–9; C M Dixon pp10, 18, 20; Colorific! M Brooke p27; Corbis: R Wood p11, M Nicholson p25, C & J Lenars p26; Werner Forman Archive: British Museum p12, Egyptian Museum, Cairo pp16, 22–3.

Cover photograph reproduced with permission of Werner Forman Archive, Egyptian Museum, Cairo.

Special thanks to Paul Flux and Jane Shuter for their comments in the preparation of this book.

Every effort to contact copyright holders of any material reproduced in this book. Any omissions will be rectified in subsequent printings if notice is given to the publisher.

Cover picture:
Tutankhamon's throne, about 1330 B.C., wood covered with gold leaf and silver, inlaid with colored glass and semi-precious stones.

This relief on the back panel of Tutankhamon's throne shows the young pharaoh with his wife, Ankhesenamun. She is smoothing perfumed oil on her husband's broad collar from a small cup in her hand. The rays of the sun god, Amon, shine down on them. This picture is unusual for Egyptian standards. Tutankhamon is almost lolling on his throne, and his queen is shown as the same color and height as he is. Most Egyptian art followed strict rules and did not try to make people look natural and relaxed.

Words that appear in the text in bold, **like this**, are explained in the glossary on page 31.

CONTENTS

WHAT WAS EGYPTIAN ART?

Ancient Egypt was full of brilliant colors. Under the blue sky was the silver Nile River, the red, orange, and brown earth, golden sands, and green grass. Ancient Egyptian art reflects these colorful surroundings. By studying the art, we can discover how the people lived, worked, and what they believed in. Most of the Egyptian art that has survived has to do with their religious beliefs. Much of it, such as tomb paintings, mummy cases, models, and statues, are related to their dead. The ancient Egyptians believed that people came back to life after they had died.

Winnowing corn, part of a wall painting from the tomb of Nakht, about 1320 B.C.

*This wall painting comes from the tomb of the royal **scribe**, Nahkt. It tells us about his life. Here, his servants are separating (winnowing) corn. The **composition** of the painting is well balanced with the standing figures on both sides framing the action. Egyptian paintings are like colorful diagrams.*

Three kingdoms

Ancient Egyptian history is divided into three main periods: the Old Kingdom (about 2686–2181 B.C.), Middle Kingdom (about 2040–1782 B.C.) and New Kingdom (about 1570–1070 B.C.). The wall painting on page 4 was painted during the Middle Kingdom. Art did not change much over 3000 years, but there were some differences between the art of each period.

Little pictures

Artists also had to learn to write. The early form of Egyptian writing was made up of tiny pictures. Even writing was an art form in ancient Egypt.

*Katep and his wife Hetepheres, from Giza, about 2300 B.C., height 19 in., **limestone**.*

This statue was made during the Old Kingdom. It follows the ancient Egyptian rules of art. The figures' hands are on their knees. The wife's skin is pale yellow while her husband's is red. Facial details were always painted in black.

Rules of art

The layout of all art was important. Nothing was left to chance. Everything was measured and put in its place for a purpose. All art—statues, paintings, and buildings—obeyed rules of balance and **proportion**. Every artist had to learn the rules. For example, statues of seated people had to have their hands on their knees. Statues of men had to have darker skin than statues of women. Gods had special features and were often shown with the heads of particular animals.

5

MATERIALS AND METHODS

Egyptian boys usually followed the same profession as their parents. Women and girls were not expected to have a profession; they cared for the home. But if a craftsman had no sons, he could teach his profession to his daughters. All artists were seen as craftsmen. They trained from as young as five years old in workshops alongside other craftsmen, such as sculptors and jewelers.

One man, who was like a chief designer, supervised them all. He planned their work and checked that the standards were high. Most of the work followed a traditional pattern. Occasionally a fresh design was demanded, for example, when a new pharaoh (king) came to the throne.

Jewelers at work, part of a wall-painting from the tomb of Nebamun at Thebes, about 1400 B.C.

Paintings give information. This shows us jewelers in the craftsmen's workshop. The artists who painted this had a good sense of design and color. Although it seems a simple picture, it is well balanced and includes plenty of detail. What do you think the jewelers are doing?

Egyptian artists did not sign their art because they worked in teams. If an artist was particularly skillful at copying past work and handling materials, he might be given more work. But usually only the supervisor, or chief designer, became well known.

Preparing paints, brushes, and surfaces

Brushes of different sizes were made from lengths of coarse palm leaves or knotted rope that had been beaten at one end, so that they formed stiff brushes. Paint was made from finely ground minerals mixed with vegetable gum or egg. It gave a smooth finish. This kind of paint is called **tempera**. If a stone or wood surface was too rough to paint on, it was coated first with a layer of chalky liquid that dried to make a hard, smooth surface. **Compositions** were drawn with the help of a grid, marked out in red, to make sure that everything was of the right **proportion**.

Painter's brush and palette with minerals found in Thebes, about 1450–1250 B.C. The length of the palette is about 5 inches.

The coarse-haired brush is still clogged with red paint. Three pieces of colored rock are on the palette with a grinder. Artists ground the rocks into powder ready to mix and use as paint.

ART AND THE AFTERLIFE

The ancient Egyptians believed that when a person died, their spirit left their body, but came back later and lived an afterlife. This meant that the body had to be preserved so that the returning spirit could use it. So, the person had to be buried with all the items they might need in the afterlife.

Preserving the body

The Egyptians preserved the body by **embalming** it. To do this, first they removed internal organs which would cause the body to decay.

These were stored in containers called canopic jars. Then they dried out the body by soaking it in a salty liquid for about 40 days. Next, they wrapped the body in bandages to make a mummy. The mummy was put into a mummy-shaped coffin (sarcophagus). The wealthy people had more care taken over them. Important people had more than one sarcophagus, which they stacked inside each other.

Painting on Djedbastinfanth's wooden coffin, at El Hiba, after 600 B.C.

These scenes show bodies being prepared for burial. The painting is like a diagram. Each section shows different stages in the process. The objects either side of the dogs, above the mummy, are canopic jars. The colors would have been much brighter when the coffin was first painted.

Art for the afterlife

People were buried with items they would need for the afterlife, such as food, furniture, and clothing. They also included models of houses, boats, servants, and animals, which would change from models to the real thing in the afterlife. Again, the more important people had extra items buried with them. The craftsmen who made the models could produce simple clay models, or complicated and magnificently painted models, depending on how much they were paid!

Serving girl, about 1900 B.C., height 16 in., wood.

This little servant girl is ready to serve her master or mistress in the afterlife. She is carrying a basket on her head containing bread and meat.

SIGNS AND SYMBOLS

About 5,000 years ago Egyptian **scribes** began drawing simple pictures to represent objects and sounds. This was one of the first forms of writing. They wrote on **papyrus scrolls** using colored inks and pens made from the softened ends of reeds.

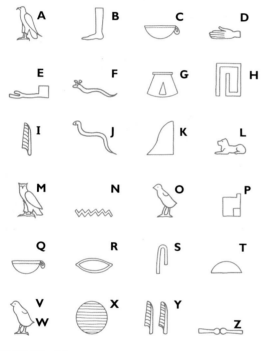

Egyptian writing

Gradually words were built up out of several different signs. To clarify the meaning of a word, a picture of the object or action was sometimes added at the end. This picture writing, called **hieroglyphics**, was used for religious writings and for **inscriptions** on monuments. There were about 750 different hieroglyphs. Most are pictures of people, animals, plants, or objects. It took about twelve years to learn to write in the Egyptian script. Many artists and scribes (one person often did both jobs) started learning at the age of four!

From the papyrus of Hunefer, at Thebes, about 1320 B.C., height 16 in.

The scene of priests and mourners at the entrance to Hunefer's tomb shows burial rituals in signs and symbols. The jackal-headed priest supports the mummy as Hunefer's wife, Nesha, and another woman mourn him. Behind stands the priest in charge, wearing a leopard skin. Other priests, painted in different shades of brown, make offerings.

Relief, inside the tomb of Queen Nefertari, about 1250 B.C., **limestone**.

The colors in this relief are still bright, having been preserved by the dry climate. Queen Nefertari was the wife of a great king, Ramses II.
The hieroglyphs mean: "Words spoken by the Osirified Great Royal Wife Nefertari, beloved of Mut." (Osirified means dead and now a goddess; Mut was the wife of the god Amon-Ra, king of the gods.)

Make a mummy and a message card

Materials:

thin poster board   paper
felt-tipped pens   paints
scissors   glue

1. Fold a piece of paper in half, lengthways. Along the fold draw and cut out the shape of half a mummy. Make cuts side-by-side from the folded edge, out to the mummy outline, leaving an uncut border ¾ inch wide.

Gently bend the cut strips backwards and forwards.

2. Carefully open out the paper. Pinch the borders at the top and bottom of the mummy and push out the strips.

3. Paint around the mummy. Cut to size a piece of poster board and fold in half lengthways. Glue the mummy on to it. Write your own hieroglyphic message on the card.

PAINTING TECHNIQUES

The most important Egyptian paintings were on the walls of temples, tombs, and palaces. But the Egyptians also painted on **papyrus**.

Plans and grids

Wall paintings were made to a strict plan. First, plaster was smoothed over uneven walls. Then an outline artist would mark it with a grid of squares, using string soaked in paint. A trainee artist would draw in the scene, copying from a picture on papyrus. Last of all, painters would fill in the outlines with bright colors.

Wall painting from the tomb of Nebanom, Thebes, about 1356 B.C., height 38 in.

This wall painting gives plenty of information about fish, birds, plants, and also hunting methods.

Flat pictures

People look flat and strange in Egyptian paintings because they were painted in a particular way. Important people were painted larger than others. Heads were shown from the side, because this was clearer than a face-on view. Eyes and the top half of the body were shown from the front, but arms and legs were shown from the side, so that they were easier to see. A foot was always shown from the inner side. Men were painted a reddish-brown color, while women were pale yellow.

The artists did not really think that people looked like this. They were following rules. Their paintings had messages in them, instead of being lifelike portraits. Egyptian artists followed these rules for nearly 3,000 years.

Paint palette

Brightly colored paints used by the Egyptians were made from ground up minerals. Yellow, red, and brown came from soil. White came from crushed **limestone**. Green was a mixture of blue powdered copper and yellow soil. Black came from soot, and blue came from a semiprecious stone called **lapis lazuli**. Sometimes gold dust was used as paint, too.

ART FOR THE GODS

Gods and goddesses were important to all Egyptians. The Egyptians believed that they controlled life, death, and the natural world. Wall paintings in the tomb of Thutmose III show 700 Egyptian gods. The most important were Ra, the sun god, and Osiris, the god of the afterlife.

The Judgment of Hunefer from the Book of the Dead, about 1320 B.C.

The Book of the Dead was a book that was buried in tombs with the dead. This painting shows the jackal-headed god Anubis leading Hunefer to the scales where his heart will be weighed against a feather from the goddess of truth. If the heart is lighter than the feather, then he passes the test. If it is heavier, then Ammut (the crocodile-headed creature under the scales) will eat him. The ibis-headed god, Thoth, writes down the result. Then Hunefer is led by falcon-headed Horus to Osiris. He has passed the test! Notice how skillfully the artist has painted Hunefer's semi-transparent clothes.

Animal features

As you can see, the Egyptians believed that gods and goddesses could take on the form of a particular bird or animal. Some had the body of a human and the head of an animal or bird, such as Anubis the jackal, and Horus the falcon. Every artist had to know what each god and goddess looked like.

Palaces of the gods

A temple was the palace of a god. The ruling pharaoh would order a temple to be built for a particular god or goddess. A statue of the god was made for its spirit to live in. Only the high priests could see the statue for fear of insulting the god, so it had to be hidden in a shrine. Priests would offer this statue perfumes, clothing, and food. Ordinary people also came with offerings.

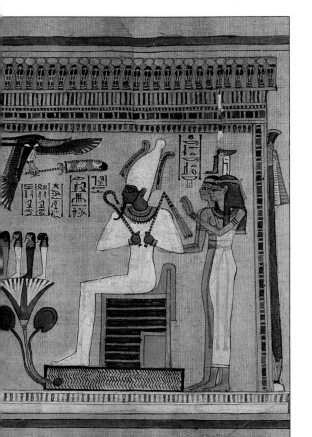

Artists and craftsmen were always needed to make art for the gods. They built and decorated temple and tomb walls. They also made statues of the gods and goddesses and painted stories about them on **papyrus**. Artists and craftsmen often worked deep in the darkness of tombs and temples. Their only light was from candle-type lamps or from **bronze** mirrors that reflected sunlight into the tomb.

ART FOR THE KING

As we have seen, the Egyptians believed in many gods. These gods affected different parts of people's lives. The pharaoh, king of Egypt, was also seen as a god. He was not as important as some of the other gods, but he was not just a human either. Because of this, pharaohs had to be obeyed, even if people did not want to do as a pharaoh ordered. The pharaoh Amenhotep IV (1350–34 B.C.) changed people's beliefs and artistic practices for at least as long as he lived.

A different belief

Amenhotep IV believed in worshiping just one god, the sun god called Aton. He changed his name to Akhenaton in honor of this god. He built a new capital city, Akhetaton, and moved there. We are not sure if he told people that they were not allowed to worship the other gods that he had rejected. But we do know that many people followed Amenhotep's beliefs because he was their pharaoh.

*King Akhenaton with his wife and three of their daughters, from Amarna, about 1350 B.C., 13 by 15½ in., **limestone** relief.*

King Akhenaton and Queen Nefertiti are sitting on stools, relaxing with their daughters. The sun god, Aton, shines down on them all. Kings had never been shown in natural poses like this before.

A closer look

Look closer at the relief opposite. Akhenaton's daughters may seem unnatural and rather like tiny adults instead of small children, but they are pictured almost front-facing. Now look at Akhenaton's feet—you can see his toes! This shows an interest in making the images look three dimensional, instead of flat, like the set forms of traditional Egyptian art.

A different art

Akhenaton believed that art should be more lifelike. He encouraged artists to forget the rules of painting and show things as they really·are. Again, we do not know if he forced artists to change their ways, but if anyone wanted to work for him, they would have to work the way he wished. As soon as Akhenaton died, artists went back to the old rules.

Wall painting from the tomb of Nebamon at western Thebes, about 1356 B.C., height 24 in.

Look at the musicians as they entertain guests at a meal. Compare their faces, bodies, hands, and feet.

RELIEF ART

Egyptian paintings were smooth and flat, but artists also made raised pictures called **reliefs**. Sculptors carved the reliefs. During the Old and Middle Kingdoms reliefs were usually in soft **limestone**. In the New Kingdom they were often in **sandstone**.

About 1900 B.C., painted relief.

This colored relief of the nobleman Imn-n-hat and his wife shows them seated on a bench with their son, Intef, between them. Nearby is a table piled high with food. Egyptians liked to show scenes from family life. Reliefs followed the same rules as paintings. The backgrounds were usually gray or yellow.

Colored carvings

Granite, **alabaster**, limestone, sandstone and richly colored rocks were cut out of **quarries** near the Nile River to be used for building and carving. Next to the reliefs, sculptors also carved detailed and precise **inscriptions**, and images of gods and pharaohs. Any mistakes were filled in with plaster.

There were two kinds of reliefs. Raised reliefs had the main subjects standing out from the background. Sunken reliefs had the main subjects cut into the surface, with the background standing out. Sunken reliefs are usually on outside walls where there is strong sunlight, or on monuments and pillars.

Reliefs show every kind of activity, from farming to feasting, from jewelry-making to dancing. Some of the scenes follow a sequence, showing how a task or activity was done, and some have a message.

How relief artists worked

Relief artists worked in the same way as painters. First they dipped a string in red paint and stretched it across the stone vertically and horizontally to make a grid. Then they carefully drew in the outline. Once the drawing had been finished and had been approved by the supervisor, specialist stone cutters took over. After the picture had been carved, artists painted it with brilliant colors to make it stand out even more.

Servants bringing offerings to Ptah-hotep, Saqqara, about 2450 B.C., limestone, height of each figure, 17 in.

Many bold reliefs like this were found in the tomb of Ptah-hotep, an important man who worked for the king. The figures, although set in the usual Egyptian style, appear to be moving as they carry their offerings of lotus flowers, livestock, and food.

SECRETS OF SCULPTURE

This bust of Queen Nefertiti, wife of Akhenaton, was found among the remains of a sculptor's studio in Tel el-Amarna. Her eyes are made from rock crystals. The statue follows the style of the more lifelike art of Akhenaton's reign.

Using simple **chisels** and **mallets**, sculptors chipped around the stone until the right shape appeared.

The statue was tied to a sledge and dragged to the Nile River. The ground was sprinkled with water to help it slide. It was put on a boat and carried to the temple or tomb it was made for. This only happened during a flood tide, when the river was at its highest. People would line the route to worship the statue as it passed.

When it reached its destination, workers polished it with sand, water, and stones covered with leather. Finally, they painted it.

Making statues

Sculptors worked close to the **quarries**. With the help of the **stonemasons**, they found a suitable block of stone. Other artists marked the stone with a grid and copied the outline of the statue in red or black ink from the sculptor's drawing.

Making models

Sculptors used ivory, wood, and metal as well as stone. They carved small wooden models of people doing everyday tasks to accompany a dead person on his or her journey to the next world. One Egyptian word for sculptor means "he who keeps alive."

Bronze statuettes of gods and goddesses were also made for tombs. First a model was made in beeswax and coated with clay, leaving a small hole in the base. The model was then heated to harden the clay and melt the wax, which then poured out through the hole. Next, molten bronze was poured in. When the bronze had cooled and hardened, the clay was broken, leaving the bronze model.

King Pimay, 770 B.C., height 10 in., bronze.

*This kneeling bronze statuette, from the New Kingdom, is holding two offering pots. The king's name is on the **cartouches** on his shoulders. The figure would have been placed in a tomb in front of a larger figure of a god or goddess.*

EGYPTIAN STATUES

Most statues were of gods, goddesses, pharaohs, and queens. Sculptors were skilled at carving both small and gigantic statues.

*The Great Sphinx at Giza, about 2550 B.C., 240 by 66 ft., **sandstone**.*

*Built in the Old Kingdom, this giant statue guards the great **pyramids** at Giza. Sculptors used scaffolding to carve the huge rock found in a local **quarry**. It has the body of a lion and head of a human, and is thought to represent King Khafre. It is the largest free-standing sculpture that survives from the ancient world.*

Statue stories

It is said that a young prince once rested against the head of the Great Sphinx when its body was covered in sand. The sun god appeared and promised to make him king if he freed the Sphinx from the sand. The prince did so, and became Thutmose IV.

The largest known statue ever to be cut from a single block of **granite** stood in the temple of a king known as Ramses the Great. Fragments of an even larger Egyptian statue have been found, including a big toe that is the size of a person.

Symbols of life

Statues, like paintings and **reliefs**, were not meant to copy nature. They were meant to be **symbols**. Sculptors followed strict rules. Statues were always youthful figures. Men stood with the left foot forward, arms by their sides, or seated on a throne. Women stood or sat rigidly. Most statues were painted, symbolizing the colorfulness of the world.

Tutankhamon's tomb

The tomb of a particularly rich Egyptian pharaoh was discovered in the 1920s. It was that of Tutankhamon (King Akhenaton's younger brother). Tutankhamon became pharaoh after Akhenaton. Tutankhamon died when he was eighteen. In his tomb were priceless treasures, including jewelry, weapons, and furniture covered with gold and decorations of semiprecious stones.

The mask of Tutankhamon, found in a tomb in the Valley of the Kings, dated about 1330 B.C., height 22 in., gold, glass, and semiprecious stones.

This mask, made from 242 lbs of gold, covered the face of Tutankhamon's mummy. On the forehead are the vulture-goddess of Upper Egypt and the serpent-goddess of Lower Egypt. All pharaohs used these symbols to show that they ruled both parts of Egypt. All pharaohs also wore a false "beard" for ceremonies.

EGYPTIAN BUILDINGS

Like Egyptian paintings, buildings were of **geometric** design. Temples were built of stone so they would last for ever. Houses and palaces were made of mud bricks, mixed with grit and straw, shaped and hardened in the sun.

Brilliant colors

Palaces and wealthy people's houses had high windows to let in air and light, but to keep the inside cool. Walls, floors, and ceilings were coated in plaster, then painted white or tiled in brilliant colors. Some walls had wall paintings called murals. Gardens with pools surrounded some houses, but most people relaxed on the flat roofs.

Detail from the Book of the Dead, about 1320 B.C., paint on papyrus.

The royal **scribe**, *Nakht, and his wife, Tjiui, stand in front of their typical Egyptian house.*

Furniture for the wealthy

Only rich Egyptians could furnish their houses with chairs, beds, chests, and tables, probably carved from local fig wood. Chairs were a sign of wealth. Houses also had painted wall hangings. The pharaoh and nobles had furniture made of costly ebony or cedar wood, inlaid with gold or precious stones.

Homes for the gods

The ruling pharaoh ordered temples to be built in honor of gods or goddesses. **Architects** designed them, drawing plans and making small models first for the pharaoh to approve.

An amazing temple

During the New Kingdom, Ramses II ordered an amazing temple to be built. Stonecutters hollowed out the **sandstone** cliff, leaving pillars in place as ceiling supports. Sculptors carved eight pillars into statues, 33 foot tall, of Ramses, and four giant seated figures of him guarding the temple entrance.

Painters then added colors and decorated the walls with hieroglyphs and **reliefs**. They always followed the strict rules of temple decoration. Twice a year, on Ramses' birthday and the anniversary of his coronation, the rising sun reached the innermost part of the temple, lighting up the statues of Ramses and the god Amon.

*This was the forecourt of the temple of the god Amon-Ra, at Karnak, 2000–1000 B.C., sandstone, **limestone** and **granite**.*

Every Egyptian temple had a sacred lake. This temple was big enough to hold several modern cathedrals. The statue is 50 ft. high.

25

THE POWERFUL PYRAMIDS

Pharaohs' tombs

The most famous Egyptian buildings are the **pyramids**, built as tombs for pharaohs. Pyramids were not built through all of the ancient Egyptian period (which lasted from about 3000 B.C. to 30 B.C.). Pharaohs were also buried in other kinds of tombs.

Pyramid building took place from about 2700 B.C. to 2400 B.C., during the Old Kingdom. These pyramids are famous for several reasons. First, they are some of the few remaining ancient Egyptian structures. Second, they were magnificently decorated. We get much of our information about ancient Egypt from the paintings and carvings in the pyramids. Third, pyramids make us wonder about their construction and purpose.

*The Great Pyramid at Giza, about 2660 B.C., height 530 ft., **sandstone**.*

*The most famous and largest of all pyramids is the Great Pyramid of King Khufu, or Cheops. It was once covered with gleaming white **limestone** and the top was capped with shining gold. It is one of the Seven Wonders of the ancient world.*

Stairways to heaven

No one really knows why the Egyptians buried their kings in tombs of this shape. The first pyramid to be built was not smooth-sided, but built with giant steps. Some people believe pyramids represented giant steps to heaven. Most later pyramids were made with smooth sides. No one really knows exactly how pyramids were built.

The largest pyramid of all contains 2,000,000 blocks of stone, each weighing about the same as a large bus. Each block was moved without any machinery. All workers had were wooden rollers, ropes and pulleys, and **bronze** tools for cutting. Yet all the blocks fit together so closely that you cannot fit a piece of paper between any of them. They must have taken many people many years to build.

Seeing in the dark

It is remarkable that Egyptian art is so exact, colorful, and skillful, when most of it was made in the gloomy darkness of tombs.

Step Pyramid of King Zoser at Saqqara, about 2630 B.C., height 213 ft., sandstone.

This is one of the oldest stone structures in Egypt. It was designed by Imhotep, a royal **architect** and high priest of the sun god.

THE BEGINNINGS OF MODERN DESIGN

Ancient Egyptian art was so carefully worked out and organized that it has a power which can still be seen today. The artists were mostly anonymous (names unknown), producing work mainly for religious purposes, not decoration. They could not express themselves freely like artists can today. They had to be exact, showing nature in a set way. They could never ignore the rules.

A wall-painting from a tomb in Thebes, about 1400 B.C., 25 in.

Painted in the New Kingdom, this shows nature in the simplest way. Like a map, the pond is flat-looking, shown from above, so that you can see the fish, birds, and plants. Trees, to be clear, are shown from the side.

Art forever

Ancient Egyptian art was made for eternity. In a way the artists achieved that aim. Their work has lasted and influenced others for centuries. The ancient Greeks and Romans copied their **techniques** and ways of showing nature for years. **Scribes** in the Middle Ages copied their illustrated **papyrus** designs, to make beautiful decorated books. In the early 1900s, a style of art and design called Art Deco used some of the ancient Egyptians' flat, **geometric compositions**.

Art Deco

In 1922, the discovery of Tutankhamon's tomb created a new interest in Egyptian art. Designers who were already developing a new style called Art Deco began adding Egyptian-looking touches to their designs. This suited the style well. Like ancient Egyptian art, Art Deco could be applied to all art, from paintings and sculpture, to furniture and buildings. Designers combined bright colors with geometric shapes, but used modern materials.

Graphic design

Hieroglyphics have also been a great influence on **graphic design**. Look out for signs and **symbols** that could be modern hieroglyphs, like road signs and washing instructions.

New or old? Is this a modern design, or was it painted about 4,000 years ago?

It is, in fact, a detail from the inside of the wooden coffin of a doctor named Seni. It was made in about 2000 B.C. Artists have been learning from balanced compositions like this for over 4,000 years.

TIME LINE

B.C.

3500	Development of **hieroglyphs**.
2686–2134	OLD KINGDOM Step **Pyramid** built for King Zoser. Great Pyramids and Sphinx built at Giza.
2300	Statue made of Katep and Hetepheres.
2040–1640	MIDDLE KINGDOM
1552–1085	NEW KINGDOM
1450	The priest Nakht dies and detailed paintings of his life are painted in his tomb.
1400	Amenemheb dies and his tomb is filled with paintings for the afterlife.
1356	Nebamun dies, and the artists decorate his tomb in a more natural way than before.
1350–34	Akhenaton rules with his wife Nefertiti. He makes everyone worship one god, tries to make art more realistic, and has a new capital built called Akhetaton.
1333–23	Tutankhamon (Akhenaton's half-brother) rules, bringing back the old gods, the old capital at Thebes, and the old rules of art.
1323	A tomb, sarcophagus, golden mask, and many other precious works of art are made for Tutankhamon's burial.
1320	The Royal scribe Nakht dies. A beautiful **papyrus** book is made for his spirit to take to the afterlife.
1304–1237	Ramses II rules. He has a temple built at Abu Simbel and one restored at Karnak.
1250	Ramses II has a tomb built for his favorite wife, Queen Nefertari. It has huge statues outside of the two of them. The inside is decorated with elaborate messages and **reliefs**. Sennedjem, an important man, dies. His tomb is filled with colorful pictures of his life on earth.
1070	Egypt becomes less powerful. The kingdom is split into two areas and they fight each other. Because they are wealthy, both kingdoms are attacked by many other countries. Many of the royal tombs are broken into and robbed.
	The Romans have more influence. Egyptian art is changed forever.

GLOSSARY

alabaster Translucent (slightly see-through) creamy-white stone.

architect Someone who designs a building and makes sure that it is properly built is an architect.

bronze Brownish-gold metal made from a mixture of copper and tin. It is hard wearing and easy to work with.

cartouches These are oval rings enclosing the (hieroglyphic) name and title of a king.

chisel A metal tool with a shaped tip.

composition The way things are arranged in a picture, so that the finished layout looks organized.

geometric This is a type of design using lines and shapes.

granite This is a hard gray stone.

graphic design Drawing, painting, and arranging words, usually for magazines, television, or advertising.

hieroglyphics This is a form of picture writing. The word means "sacred carving" in ancient Greek.

inscriptions These are words carved or marked on a monument or stone.

limestone Gray or creamy-white rock that is fairly soft and easy to carve.

mallet A wooden hammer used to hit the end of a chisel when carving.

papyrus This is a marsh plant and the paper made from it.

proportion When something is in proportion, it is of a correct balance and size.

pyramid A building with triangular sides which rise up from a square base and meet together at the top.

quarries Places where stone is taken out of the ground are called quarries.

reliefs Scenes carved in stone or wood.

sandstone A rock made of sand, usually red, yellow, brown, gray or white.

scribes Ancient writers and artists.

scrolls Layers of papyrus, pressed together and then rolled up. Scrolls were then often many yards long.

stonemasons These are people who cut, shape, and build with stone.

symbol A simplified sign, shape, or object that represents something else.

techniques Ways of doing things.

tempera This is paint made of color mixed with egg.

MORE BOOKS TO READ

Defrates, Joanna. *What Do We Know About the Egyptians?* New York: Peter Bedrick Books, 1992.

Pearson, Anne. *Everyday Life in Ancient Egypt.* Danbury CT: Watts, 1994.

Rees, Rosemary. *The Ancient Egyptians.* Crystal Lake IL: Heinemann Library, 1997.

INDEX

Numbers in plain type (24) refer to the text.
Numbers in bold type (28) refer to an illustration.